A Writer's Reference

with Exercises